Jesus
Touching
Others

Discovery House Publishers

Books, music, and videos that feed the soul with the Word of God

Box 3566 Grand Rapids, MI 49501

The Friendship Connection

Jesus Touching Others

Norene Antin

Friendship Circle® International

Discovery House Publishers is affiliated with RBC Ministries, Grand Rapids, Michigan 49512

Discovery House books are distributed to the trade exclusively by Barbour Publishing, Inc., Uhrichsville, Ohio 44683

All Scripture quotations, unless otherwise indicated, are from the HOLY BIBLE, NEW INTERNATIONAL VERSION® (NIV®). Copyright © 1973, 1978, 1984 by International Bible Society. Used by permission of Zondervan Publishing House.

Scripture quotations noted *The Message* are from *The Message*. Copyright © 1993, 1994, 1995. Used by permission of Nav Press Publicity Group.

In some cases, names and details have been changed in the "Modern Day Story" out of respect for and in protection of individuals.

Library of Congress Cataloging-in-Publication Data

Antin, Norene.
    Jesus touching others / by Norene Antin.
        p. cm. -- (The friendship connection)
    ISBN 1-57293-074-8
    1. Christian women--Religious life. 2. Women in the Bible. 3. Friendship--Religious aspects--Christianity. I. Title.
    BV4527 .A58 2001
    248.8'4 43--dc21

2001028321

Printed in the United States of America.

01 02 03 04 05 06 07 / CHG / 7 6 5 4 3 2 1

contents . . .

acknowledgments . . .

God is worthy of unending thanks and praise for the way He has orchestrated the writing, formatting, and publication of this study guide. It is my prayer that it will be used to bring much glory and honor to His name!

Second, my thanks go to my husband, Ernie, who is my greatest fan and whose humor, faithfulness, and prayers continue to reflect God's amazing grace and friendship to me.

Many have contributed to the formation and publication of this study guide. It has long been on my heart to create this guide as a tool for the ministry of Friendship Circle®. Because of several women who have in loving service come alongside the women in Friendship Circle®, I have had the time I've needed. In particular, I want to thank Sandi Nightingale, Annie Hurley, Carole Veitch, and Cheryle Hamilton. I am grateful to Cheryle and to Judy Burkhalter who made possible the first version of this work.

Others who have cheered me on include Heather Webb, Kristi Curtis, Mario and Susan Ferrante, Gen Rideout, Sue Arestad, Mary Jane Apple, and my daughter, Vanessa Antin.

Without Rosalie Harkless this present work would not have materialized. She has artistically designed, expertly edited, creatively composed, and diligently typeset—all with a Christlike spirit. Thank you, Rosalie, for your labor of love.

how to use this study guide . . .

This guide is designed to be used in a group setting. Although it is formatted as a Bible study, its emphasis is chiefly on Bible application. Therefore, there are no Bible study questions to answer, but rather discussion questions, testimonies and helpful suggestions for reflection before and during group sharing time. There is also a section designated for prayer needs and praises. Prayer is the vital link with God that will help you to gain maximum benefit from this study.

You will need a Bible to look up the primary Scripture passages for each lesson; otherwise most references are quoted, along with explanations where needed. However, the Spirit may prompt you to look deeper into a particular passage, or even to look up another reference altogether. Therefore, it will be helpful for added depth of understanding to have your Bible open before you as you reflect upon and discuss the material. You will certainly also need an open heart to listen to what the Spirit is saying to you.

Each chapter begins with a poem or quotation, followed by a Scripture reference or references and a story/character sketch focusing on an individual in some way connected with Jesus during His earthly life. A related contemporary story reinforces the main theme of the lesson. "Sharing Our Hearts" discussion starters are open-ended topics and questions designed to promote fellowship and self-discovery. "A Change of Heart," a lesson summary and application section, helps to bring home the main point and "Walk the Word" suggests specific ways in which you can apply the lesson to your life, helping to make your study both personal and profitable. This feature is sometimes followed by a poem, anecdote or quotation. For additional meditation during the week(s) following the lesson, brief topical Scripture references are provided in the section, "Hearing His Heart."

The last section of the guide is a prayer journal to record petitions as well as praises for answers received—a powerful tool that will knit hearts together as you come face-to-face with the grace of the Lord Jesus Christ.

The unique design of this study guide is based on the tools used in the ministry of Friendship Circle® International. This is a Bible-based group that gathers for the purpose of developing and cultivating friendships with the Lord Jesus and with each other. If you would like more information, please contact: Friendship Circle® International, P.O. Box 2062, Renton, WA 98056.

CHAPTER 1

Snapshots In My Life

A Friend Shares

To A New Friend

*G*od knew that I was all alone,
Strange in a strange new land.
Knew there was none to share my load,
To care and understand;
He knew the road was rough and steep,
That helping hands were few.
He knew my heart, and all its needs
And so He sent me you.

He sent me you. Your way was new
And long and lonesome, too,
So you could understand my need
And I was kin to you.
God knew each load would weigh but half
If it were shared by two;
He knew the strength of fellowship
And so He sent me you.

Together now we journey on,
Together praise and pray,
Together love and laugh and live,
Together seek His way.
Now holds the road so lonely once
A glory sweet and new
For Jesus closer drew Himself
The day He sent me you!

—Margaret Clarkson

Looking back, I can see that these events which seemed so difficult at the time have now fallen into place. I realize that God brought me through these things to make me who I am, and to bring me to the place where I am more sensitive to others' needs and not so worried about meeting my own. A fruitful ministry of friendship, that I believe pleases God, has resulted.

ver a decade ago, I found myself co-teaching a women's class at the church I attended. Little did I realize that my life was going to be radically changed, because what occurred week after week led me down a path that has brought about a relationship with God and His people that has profoundly impacted my life.

Allow me to back up further. Several years prior to my teaching, my husband and I were in full-time professional ministry in a church. Through a series of unwelcome events, we were dismissed from that church. This experience was devastating for me, and I determined that I would never again return to involvement with church people. I kept that vow for seven years, but at a great personal cost. I was emotionally and spiritually starved, developed physical illnesses, and found myself friendless. But it was in that weakened state that I finally allowed God's love to soften my heart. Through what I now recognize as His hand of mercy, He brought me back. He showed me my own folly of focusing on others' sins and shortcomings more than on my own, and I made a commitment to trust God every day.

It was at that time that I began to mull over in my mind the question, "If Jesus were alive today, what form would He take?" Two thousand years ago, He had come as a babe, grown up and lived among a relatively small group of people, preached, taught, and healed. But I could not see or touch Him today in any concrete way. What tangible form would He take if He were to "show up"?

One day it dawned on me that this question itself was flawed. Instead of asking "*If* Jesus *were* alive, what form would he take," I needed to ask "*Since* Jesus *is* alive, what form is He taking?" I glimpsed then the mystery of the church, which He has called His Bride. How much He loves her! He indeed was very much alive and active in my world even then through this holy and yet human institution, despite all her imperfections. The *church* was Christ with "skin on."

It was not much later that I was teaching the women's class and began this incredible journey of seeing God at work in His people. The real experience began when some of the women started to approach me individually to ask whether I would have time to meet them for coffee. Each of them had something to share and what they shared were unbelievable stories—astonishing even to someone who had been raised in a preacher's home and had "heard it all." They were stories of intense heartache, and my own heart went out to them. I was moved to help them, but I did not know how to do any more than I was already doing in my weakened state, still focused as I was on trying to regain my own health and solve my own problems. In my concern for these women, though, I cried out to God for help, asking Him, "What can I do?"

In all honesty, my first inclination was to do nothing, to allow each of them to find her own help and solutions. I had a family to raise and a weekly ministry for which to prepare. But my next thought was that I really cared deeply about these women. In a short time they had become very dear to me. They were my friends, and because I greatly valued them I could not ignore them and their needs. Friends, like God's Word, live on forever in our hearts. To give my friends a higher priority in my life was for me the only honorable path to take.

This was also an act of repentance. I had behaved so poorly in that area for so many years that ignoring them was really not an option. I just needed to figure out how to honor them. From that day forward, love took over. The issue was no longer *if* God and I could help them, but *how* He and I could work together as a team to bring about the "impossible" and meet many of their needs.

Identifying God and myself as a team seemed presumptuous to me at the time. But as I look back, I see that this relationship is not only profoundly real but also intensely powerful. It releases faith that enables me to receive from God the blessing He wants to bestow, and it gives me freedom to act as God has gifted me for His eternal purposes. God, along with any of us who receives His Son, are in a dynamic partnership.

So from that day on, my question was not "How am I going to help people?" but "How can God and I together love these friends of His, who have now become my friends too?" At first, I thought the answer was going to be a superbly developed Bible study and a women's ministry to challenge them on an intellectual level to become disciple-makers. But as I walked alongside these women, meeting them at their workplaces, sitting with them in hospital waiting rooms or next to hospital beds, or bringing a pizza to their emotionally (and sometimes physically) empty homes, I realized that they needed something more than just a Bible study and a well-prepared lesson on Sunday morning. They needed God's Word fleshed out in skin all week long.

This insight was not really so profound. It was actually quite simple and obvious. The carrying out of the mission, though, was more significant. It was, in fact, impossible to do in my own strength. Recognizing this was the beginning of my openness to God's miracle of provision, as I began to lean heavily on Him to do what I could not do by myself.

These were His people, the sheep of His pasture. He would shepherd and care for them exactly as His faithful heart of compassion longed to do. I was simply offering myself as one of many vessels He could use where and when He wanted. Therein was the secret. I was just one. There were many others who could join together with God and me in this awesome and privileged venture. I just needed to invite, identify, and train these others who could help. I did, and they responded.

They are still responding. God is still speaking to His people through His Word, through the Holy Spirit, and through His Bride, the church. Like a three-legged stool, all three are needed or life becomes lopsided. My personal experience revealed a huge imbalance in the area of Christians regularly serving as His arms and legs, voice and ears to others.

Watching my own mother struggle with the suffering and sorrows of cancer had troubled me. For decades, she had no woman her age with whom to share her agony on a regular basis because of our mistaken idea that pastors' wives are supposed to be able to handle these things on their own. I knew differently. She was as human as anyone else, and she desperately needed a kindred spirit to pray with her, laugh with her, and be the "skin" of God she could touch, especially at the time when impending death had her in its grip. I wept for her, as I still weep for other pastors' wives who suffer alone needlessly. I long to see the foolish walls that separate Christian women come down. I desire to see us do more than just study God's Word—to live out His Word on a daily basis as we walk with Him in the Spirit.

That's what Friendship Circle® is all about. And that's the purpose of this study guide—to bring us closer to God and to one another. *We are all equal at the foot of the cross.* Let the walls come down and let us begin loving and appreciating the gift of *each other* that God has given to His Bride, the church. May every assembly of the church in the world know that there is a God who befriends each member through Jesus Christ in you and in me as we offer unconditional love and start caring for each other through the vehicle of friendship.

May this study guide help you to travel in your mind and heart to places you've never been before; to see things you've never imagined; to experience faith, hope, and love you never knew existed. And when we all stand at last before His throne, having lived our lives here for a few short years, may we be confident that we have lived well, because we have loved Him well by loving each other in obedience to His Word.

"My beloved friends, let us continue to love each other since love comes from God. Everyone who loves is born of God and experiences a relationship with God. The person who refuses to love doesn't know the first thing about God, because God is love—so you can't know Him if you don't love.

This is how God showed his love for us: God sent His only Son into the world so we might live through Him. This is the kind of love we are talking about—not that we once upon a time loved God, but that He loved us and sent His Son as a sacrifice to clear away our sins and the damage they've done to our relationship with God.

My dear, dear friends, if God loves us like this, we certainly ought to love each other."

1 John 4:7-9, The Message

Yorene

Sharing Our Hearts

Discussion Starters

Reflect on the following thoughts we will discuss together. Take particular note of those that strike a chord with you and add notes in the margin about them.

1. Share some snapshots of your life. What experiences have you gone through that have enabled you to uniquely reach out to others who have experienced similar situations?

   • as a child

   • as a teenager

   • as an adult

2. Every person has a role to fill that no one else can fill in quite the same way. What is that unique calling for you, and how do you know when God is prompting you to reach out to someone else?

   ❑ to be a good listener

   ❑ to use my talent of _____
   _____

   ❑ to share my resources by _____
   _____

   ❑ to be a nurturing mom, loving sister, or understanding daughter

   ❑ other: _____
   _____

   ❑ How is God prompting me? _____

_____

_____

_____

3. In some situations, you are God's first choice to meet a need. Who have you found who has opened up to you when she wouldn't confide in anyone else?

❏ at home _____

❏ at work _____

❏ at church _____

❏ other: _____

_____

_____

4. What is holding you back from giving your unique self to others?

❏ minimizing: I feel that I don't have much to offer.

❏ fear: I'm afraid of what might happen if I do a certain thing.

❏ ignorance: I don't know what I have to give.

❏ rejection: I've been hurt, dismissed or ignored too many times.

5. What benefits do you see in walking the path God has for you?

❏ It will deepen my faith in Him.

❏ It will create in me a greater desire to love other people.

❏ It will help me to mature.

❏ It will help me to make more friends who share similar stories and interests.

❏ It will help me to see what is really important in life.

❏ other: _____

_____

_____

_____

A Change of Heart

Lesson Summary and Application

❏ I will share my unique talent with _____

_____

❏ I will offer friendship to _____

_____

❏ I will reach out in a way I never have before by _____

_____

_____

Walk the Word

❏ Share a plate of cookies with a neighbor you have never before met.

❏ Buy someone a book instead of just loaning her yours.

❏ At work or in the grocery store, notice the positive things that others do and make it a point to thank them.

Notes

A Friend In Need

"Friendship gives license to show up at the door of need without asking, 'When would you like me to come?' or 'What would you like me to do?' Nor does friendship call out, 'Just let me know if you need anything.'

"Practiced friendship whispers, 'I'll be there,' and promptly steps through the door with sensitivity, respect and understanding.

"But what about honoring the right to invite? Those who wait for parchment invitations wait long, for need rarely throws a party, rarely even has a voice.

"Yet need has its own needs. It needs protection from strangers tromping in with work boots and good intentions, and it needs relief from acquaintances wearing the spiked heels of advice and pat answers.

"Need waits with longing for the familiar entrance of dear ones who pad barefoot through the soul on ordinary days."

—Susan Lenzkes
from *A Silver Pen for Cloudy Days*
Submitted by Sharon Freeberg

Hearing His Heart

The following verses on this week's topic, "A Friend Shares," are given for deepening your love for the Lord and for others. Space is provided after each verse for you to record your thoughts.

WEEK 1

Monday

Romans 12:13

"Share with God's people who are in _____ . Practice _____ ."

_____

_____

_____

Tuesday

1 Samuel 30:24

"The _____ of the man who stayed with the supplies is to be the same as that of him who went down to battle. All will share alike."

_____

_____

_____

Wednesday

Luke 3:11

"John answered, 'The man with two tunics should _____ with him who has none, and the one who has food should do the same.'"

_____

_____

_____

Thursday

Galatians 6:6

"Anyone who receives instruction in the word must _____ _____ with his instructor."

_____

_____

_____

Friday

Hebrews 13:16

"Do not _____ and to share with others, for with such sacrifices God is pleased."

_____

_____

_____

WEEK 2

Monday

Acts 2:45-46

"Selling their _____ , they gave to anyone as he had need.... They broke bread in their homes and ate together with glad and sincere hearts, praising God and enjoying the favor of all the people."

_____

_____

_____

Tuesday

Romans 16:2

"I ask you to receive her in the LORD in a way worthy of the saints and to give her any _____ she may need from you, for she has been a great _____ to many people, including me."

_____

_____

_____

Wednesday

2 Corinthians 6:11,13

"*We have spoken freely to you ... and opened wide our hearts to you.... As a fair exchange—I speak as to my children—open wide* _____ ."

_____

_____

_____

Thursday

1 Timothy 6:17-18

"*Command those who are rich in this present world not to be arrogant nor to put their hope in wealth, which is so uncertain, but to put their hope in God, who richly provides us with everything for our enjoyment. Command them to do good, to be rich in good deeds, and to be generous and willing to* _____ ."

_____

_____

_____

Friday

2 Corinthians 9:7

"*Each man should give what he has decided in his heart to give, not* _____ *or under* _____, *for God loves a cheerful giver.*"

_____

_____

_____

CHAPTER 2

The Invisible Lady

A Friend Encourages

Guests

*P*ain knocked upon my door and said
    That she had come to stay.
And though I wouldn't welcome her
    But bade her go away
    She entered in.
Like my own shade, she followed me.
From her stabbing, stinging sword
    No moment was I free.

And then one day Another knocked
    Gently at my door.
I said, "No, pain is here;
There isn't room for more."
Then I heard His tender voice
    "It's I, be not afraid."
And from the day He entered in,
Oh, the difference He has made.

—Martha Snell Nicholson

Scripture Reading:	Mark 5:25-34
Parallel Passages:	Matthew 9:20-22,
	Luke 8:42-48

"When the teacher noticed me, that was the changing point in my life," Shannon recently told me. *"I always thought I was just a mere face that blended in with all the others in a crowded classroom, but Mr. Taylor paid attention to me in a way no one else had and it made me feel valued and respected. It was a powerful moment to have someone pick me out, name me, and be genuinely interested in me when I felt so unvalued, unnoticed, and unseen. From that day on my studies and life took on different meaning."*

hether or not we like it, we are being noticed by someone, somewhere much of the time. Although we would rather be invisible at some moments in our lives, there are other times when we crave attention—and for good reasons. Positive attention can bring about a transformation in our lives. The Invisible Lady in the Gospels, whom we will call Anna, portrays that truth vividly for us.

As the scene opens, we see "little-known and unimportant" Anna uncharacteristically interrupting a conversation. Women are not esteemed very highly in her culture. For a man to speak to a woman in public is in itself a rarity. For Anna to approach Jesus is quite a bold move on her part. How is Jesus going to handle this intrusion? Will He shame her or ignore her like others have done in the past? Will He dismiss her?

At present, Jesus the Miracle Worker is conversing with Jairus, a Very Important Person in the religious community. They are talking about a pressing, personal, life-or-death crisis that Jairus is facing. His young daughter is dying. Normally, one would not interrupt such a conversation, unless one is clueless as to what is happening—or unless she is desperate.

Desperate is probably a mild word to describe Anna. She has been an outcast, due to her bleeding condition for twelve long years. It is likely that she has lived outside the city by herself in order to protect others, including her own family, from contamination by contact with her. Anna has visited countless doctors, but rather than helping her, they have helped themselves to her pocketbook. Sadly, their medical advice has made her condition worse, rather than better.

Being poor financially is a hardship, but being bankrupt emotionally is an incredibly heavy cross to bear. On top of that, Anna has been branded unclean and untouchable due to her embarrassing illness, which probably involved some kind of menstrual disorder. There are no TV talk shows in Anna's day, and nobody discusses a subject so taboo. Anna is left to herself. She bears her secret alone, lives alone, eats alone, sleeps alone, cries alone, and nurses her scars alone. She has one lonely, painfully depressing, discouraging existence as an Invisible Lady.

That is about to change, however. Somehow Anna has heard of Jesus and devises a plan that puts her faith into action. She wants to be healed and determines that touching even a piece of the Healer's clothing will be good enough. She would not want to touch Him personally and contaminate Him, nor would she need to talk to Him. He would probably not want to converse with her, this insignificant Invisible Lady, anyway. Despite her carefully laid plans, and to her great dismay, she finds herself at this awkward moment interrupting these two important men, Jairus and Jesus.

Now interrupting anyone else is not the usual behavior for Anna. Normally, nobody is around for her *to* interrupt. Living in her insulated bubble world of isolation, Anna does not even consider that her quiet gesture might be drawing attention to herself. She had planned only to reach out and touch His garment silently and secretly—just a light touch and a hasty retreat. However, what she does not realize is that with Jesus, there are no small fixes. He specializes in the bigger, better, and forever fixes. Nothing remains small once it has come into contact with Him. Anna's plan, to sneak up behind Jesus unnoticed, fails miserably.

As Anna touches merely the hem of His garment, her fingers not even brushing against Jesus Himself, the impossible and the unexpected intersect. The impossible is that she is healed. The unexpected is that she is suddenly pulled into the limelight. All eyes are glued on her humble frame as she drops to her knees and connects with this Powerful and Knowledgeable Person, Jesus. How could He know that she had touched His garment? Only God would know something like that. Is it possible that she in her unclean state has touched *God*? What a troubling thought!

But Anna's anxiety quickly melts. In the presence of love, fear vanishes. Encouragement remains and Anonymous Anna is transformed into Darling Daughter. Yes, He calls her "daughter." He is talking to *her*—just her—to commend and encourage her. And Darling Daughter, who has for twelve years shriveled under doctors' devices, begins to blossom under Healer's hand. Not only does He heal her body; He provides nourishment for her soul as He converses tenderly with her. He has noticed her and has warmly accepted her. He has not shamed her for interrupting His plans. He has not rebuked her for sneaking up behind Him, or degraded her for being unclean or for being a woman, and He has not violated her. No. He has simply loved her.

Love encourages. It sees the gold more than the dross. It cherishes the jewel more than the stone. It hears the melody rather than the discord. It sees the heart and not the faults. It notes the quality of the china, and not the cracks.

Jesus sees, loves and listens to Anna, surprising her with compassion, touching her with tenderness, and melting her with His message, *"Daughter, your faith has healed you. Go in peace and be freed from your suffering"* (Mark 5:34). He uniquely notices her, and, in making her the only person in the Gospels whom He calls "daughter," He causes her to be forever limelighted, approved, and admired. But then, she has always been so to Him. Now though, she knows it and others see it.

Anna is healed physically and emotionally by her faith in Jesus. She is fortunate to live during this time when He is on earth. Today many people feel that God seems distant and foreign. He does not need to be. In His plan for drawing people to Himself, God often chooses to use other people to reflect His love. These individuals then become "Jesus with skin on"—His hands, arms, and feet to remind others of how much God cares for them.

A Modern Day Story
Anna: A Friend Who Is Encouraging

We sat together at Starbucks™ in a somber mood as "Anna" told me her story. "I began 'emotionally bleeding' at four years old in the home where I grew up. My dad physically, emotionally, and sexually abused me. In addition, I was told that I was a mistake and that I was not good enough or pretty enough. I have continued to bleed for years. My dad was always comparing me to others, was violent toward me, and he just plain did not want me around. Many times I thought of taking my life. I had a huge hole in my heart and I felt I was damaged beyond repair.

"Although I thought my dad had taken something from my soul I'd never get back, and I felt I would always bleed, I found out differently. About ten years ago, I met God through a friend who spent time with me and explained how God loved me and accepted me. I saw God working through her loving me just the way I was. She saw the good in me and I opened up to her and, in turn, to God. Immediately my heart started to heal and to change toward God and toward myself. I saw that I was made in His image and I was not a mistake. In fact, I was perfect in His sight. He restored my dignity, and I saw He would never remove His love from me."

Today, modern Anna is an attractive, radiant woman who displays a contagious enthusiasm and zest for living. She deeply loves people, encouraging them to be all that God created them to be. Because she sees the value of her friends' spending time with her, she is more willing to offer herself in reaching out to touch the bleeding parts of others' souls with tender compassion. Often she has been "Jesus with skin on."

Sharing Our Hearts

Discussion Starters

Reflect on the following thoughts we will discuss together. Take particular note of those that strike a chord with you and add notes in the margin about them.

1. When were you last publicly noticed or acknowledged? How did it make you feel?

   ❑ uncomfortable

   ❑ delighted

   ❑ surprised

   ❑ other: _____

   _____

2. Noticing others can help them realize their own innate value and worth. Name some things that you do to show warmth and acceptance to others, causing them to feel important. Below are some ideas:

   ❑ Be the first to greet and introduce myself.

   ❑ Smile.

   ❑ Remember their names, birthdays, etc.

   ❑ Look at them while they are talking to me.

   ❑ Allow them to interrupt my schedule.

   ❑ other: _____

   _____

   _____

   _____

3. Encouragement is like oxygen to the soul. What can you do to encourage others?

❑ Let them speak without interrupting them.

❑ Allow them to speak their mind without judging them.

❑ Compliment them on something they have done or are wearing.

❑ Ask them about themselves. Don't talk mostly about myself.

❑ other: _____

_____

4. Being vulnerable is necessary in order for a friendship to grow deeper, but it is also risky. Why are you not willing to be more open and transparent with others?

❑ I am a private person.

❑ I am afraid of of being hurt.

❑ I don't feel that I need anybody else.

❑ If people saw the real me, they would be shocked.

❑ other: _____

_____

_____

5. In what ways can you allow God to touch people through you?

❑ by praying with them

❑ by being His hands and feet to them through practical deeds

❑ by coming alongside to encourage them

❑ by asking, "What would Love do?" and then doing it

❑ maintaining a spirit of forgiveness

❑ by allowing God to use my unique gifts and talents on their behalf

❑ other: _____

_____

_____

A Change of Heart

Lesson Summary and Application

One main thought I have gleaned from the lesson:

_____

_____

_____

One application of this lesson to my life: With God's help . . .

❑ I will show warmth and acceptance by _____

_____

❑ I will seek to be more vulnerable and open to others.

❑ I will be God's hands and feet by doing the following:

_____

_____

_____

❑ I can encourage others by: _____

_____

_____

❑ other: _____

_____

Walk the Word

- ❑ Take note of the fact that someone is watching you. What do you think that person is seeing?

- ❑ Offer an encouraging word and observe the reaction.

- ❑ Observe how someone greets another warmly.

Notes

_____

_____

_____

_____

_____

_____

_____

_____

_____

_____

_____

_____

_____

_____

_____

_____

Hearing His Heart

The following verses on this week's topic, "A Friend Encourages," are given for deepening your love for the Lord and for others. Space is provided after each verse for you to record your thoughts.

Monday

1 Thessalonians 3:2-3

"We sent Timothy ... to strengthen and _____ you in your faith, so that no one would be _____ by ... trials."

_____

_____

_____

Tuesday

Hebrews 3:13

" _____ one another daily as long as it is called Today, so that none of you may be _____ by sin's deceitfulness."

_____

_____

_____

Wednesday

Romans 12:8

"If [a man's gift] is _____ , let him _____ ...."

_____

_____

_____

Thursday

Hebrews 10:25

*"Let us not give up _____ together, as some are
in the habit of doing, but let us _____ one
another—and all the more as you see the Day approaching."*

_____

_____

_____

Friday

1 Thessalonians 5:11

*"Therefore _____ and build each
other up, just as in fact you are doing."*

_____

_____

_____

WEEK 2

Monday

Acts 15:32

*"Judas and Silas, who themselves were prophets, said much to
_____ and strengthen the brothers."*

_____

_____

_____

Tuesday

Romans 15:5

*"May the God who gives endurance and _____
give you a spirit of _____ among yourselves as you
follow Christ Jesus."*

_____
_____
_____

Wednesday

Philemon 7

"Your _____ has given me great joy and encouragement, because you ... have refreshed the hearts of the saints."

_____
_____
_____

Thursday

Romans 1:11-12

"I long to see you so that I may impart to you some spiritual gift to make you strong—that is, that you and I may be _____ _____ by each other's faith."

_____
_____
_____

Friday

2 Chronicles 32:6-8

[Hezekiah] appointed military officers . . . and encouraged them with these words: 'Be _____.
Do not be afraid or discouraged because of the king of Assyria and the vast army with him, for there is a greater power with us than with him. With him is only the arm of flesh, but with us is the LORD our God to help us and to fight our battles.' And the people gained confidence from what Hezekiah the king of Judah said."

_____
_____
_____

Notes

CHAPTER 3

Jairus

A Friend Trusts

Profit and Loss

I counted dollars
while God counted crosses.
I counted gains
while He counted losses.
I counted my worth
by the things gained in store.
But He sized me up
by the scars that I bore.
I coveted honors
and sought for degrees.
He wept as He counted
the hours on my knees.
And I never knew
till one day by a grave,
How vain are these things
that we spend life to save.
That the world's truest riches
are those up above
Because we've made others
our object of love.

—quoted by Ron Jensen

Scripture Reading:	Mark 5:21-43
Parallel Passages:	Matthew 9:18-26, Luke 8:40-56

Do you find it difficult to trust? Furthermore, what determines whether someone else can be trusted? The personal relationship Jesus developed with Jairus helps answer this question for us.

"There is no amount of money or any possession that could buy back my daughter's life," John said. *"I would give everything I possess to have Sandy back."* Sandy, his daughter, had died at the young age of twenty-one of a debilitating illness, and John had buried not only his daughter but along with her part of his heart, as his candle of hope for a brighter future was snuffed out.

airus is in a similar situation to John's when he learns that his young daughter is dying. Although he is a synagogue ruler and is seen as a man of great prestige, power, and status in the community, he feels powerless as he faces this overwhelming intruder called death. He is a desperate father on a life-or-death mission, not for his synagogue, but for his family. His VIP status is unable to buy back for him what he really wants more than anything else in the world—the life of his dying daughter. And so we find him rushing to the only One he knows who can help him. Jesus is His name. Life-giving is His game. Desperately desiring life for his child, Jairus reaches out to trust this One who offers life. And just what qualifies Jairus to have his request granted?

We know what does not qualify him. As a teacher of the law, he is known for his sense of justice. He lives, sleeps, and eats rules. The teaching of rules is his native language and he is probably never more at home than when the scrolls are laid open before him so that he can tell others how to live. He is certainly happy to do so. That is his calling, you know.

But a day has come when telling others what to do doesn't work for Jairus anymore. Administering justice to others is not meeting his own grievous need or making him eligible to receive the miracle that matters. Actually, nothing is meeting his need. The situation is too hopeless, the pain too deep and agonizing, and no set of rules can glue together the broken pieces of his grieving heart. When no ladder of success is tall enough to reach the One seated on the mercy seat in heaven, desperate Jairus becomes daring Jairus, who decides that he is finished climbing ladders. It is now time to kneel. In so doing, Jairus acknowledges that faith in God qualifies him to receive healing for his daughter—if God so wills to grant it at this time.

With humble heart and bowed knee, Jairus makes his plea before this compassionate Healer and Friend and Jesus immediately responds. Mercy always responds. It says, "Let me help. I'll come with you. We're in this together" (based on Jesus' actions in Mark 5:24). And Jesus joins Jairus as he heads toward his home.

Without warning, Jairus's plan is abruptly interrupted by—of all things—a woman. Just the fact that she is a woman in this society causes her to be seen as inferior. But she is not just any woman. This one is known to be untouchable because of a serious illness. In addition to that, she has neither position nor material possessions. Oh, how totally opposite him she is. Or is she?

Now she is kneeling just where Jairus only a moment before had knelt—at the feet of Jesus. It appears that they have more in common than it seemed at first. They both need a miracle and they both have come to the only One who can perform it. Stopping to address her need, Jesus acknowledges this humble woman—another soul just like Jairus—desperate for healing.

She wanted only to touch His garment. That's all. But that is enough. Jairus watches her faith being rewarded as Jesus declares that she is not only healed, but also chosen to be His favored daughter in God's forever family of faith. Social class distinctions disappear at the feet of Jesus. Neither Jairus nor this woman is superior to or loved more than the other. Jesus' unconditional love envelopes both equally.

Patient, hopeful Jairus continues to trust Jesus as they make their way toward Jairus's home. He hardly has time to process his thoughts, for the bad-news bearers come to deliver the heart-wrenching report that the joy of his life has indeed been snuffed out. He is admonished, "Your daughter is dead. Why bother the teacher anymore?" (Mark 5:35). Bother? Has he been an annoyance to Jesus? That certainly has not been the manner in which Jesus has been treating him. Instead Jesus seems to consider these faithless ones unworthy of notice, and He deliberately ignores them. Handing Jairus the torch of truth, He rekindles this father's flickering flame of faith with the powerful words, *"Don't be afraid; just believe"* (Mark 5:36).

Jairus has a choice to make. Will he believe the eyewitness reporters, or will he believe the God who loves to disrupt funerals and make miracles from messes? The choice is not difficult when God is present with him, striding purposefully through his front door, past wailing, melancholy mourners and snickering, snooty doubters.

They both proceed to the bedside of the one who has been responsible for bringing Jairus to the feet of Jesus. Jairus and his wife keep trusting and stay close to Jesus as He takes their little girl's cold, lifeless hand. Then Jesus speaks the language of heaven. His voice of compassionate authority commands, *"Little girl, I say to you, get up"* (Mark 5:41). And she does.

Leaving strict orders *not to tell anyone* what has just transpired, the Healer instructs Jairus to feed this hungry child. Only God knows where she has been! Jesus, desiring neither fame, fanfare, nor food for Himself, quietly and unobtrusively slips out and continues on His way.

Others need to hear Mercy's voice. He carries on with purpose to make others the object of His love, both pleasing and revealing His Father, the God of all compassion, who absolutely loves to shower mercy on trusting hearts—on those who recognize that they are dry and lifeless without mercy's revitalizing breath.

Who then can be trusted? Jesus, who offers mercy and speaks truth to Jairus, is infinitely more worthy of trust than Jairus's "friends," who have merely reported facts. The marvel is that we can and must look beyond the harsh realities of our lives. We must count God into the equation, concentrating on His character and delighting in His closeness. It is true that if we stay close to Jesus, we will not only discern truth and identify our true friends, but we will ourselves be friends worth trusting.

How do we recognize Jesus' friends? He states simply that those who do what He commands are His friends (John 15:14). When we trust implicitly and love as God loves, accepting the inconvenient to attain the "impossible," we can look into the mirror and know that we are seeing someone others can trust.

A Modern Day Story
Doug, Shannon and Savannah: A Family Who Trusts

Doug and Shannon were desperate and overcome with grief. They were facing the loss of their newborn daughter due to a heart disease. Savannah's condition was indeed critical as they rushed her into the ICU of Children's Hospital for emergency open-heart surgery. Turning to God in their crisis, they trusted against all odds. What they were about to experience, only a miracle-working and merciful God could accomplish.

At least two significant experiences occurred. The first was that they were made aware of God's love for them. They saw God coming alongside them in their family, friends, and even strangers who offered love, hugs, food, and prayers. Although God was their main source of strength, these acts of love reinforced His love and helped buoy them up. The second experience was the healing of their tiny baby. As Savannah lay on the gurney waiting to be wheeled into the operating room, Shannon was aware that Another was with them in their pain.

Amazingly, Shannon was permitted to see the Person of Jesus standing beside her daughter, her tiny trusting hand enfolded in His. In the quiet of her heart, Shannon heard Him say, "Don't worry. I am with Savannah. I will hold her hand." Then Shannon watched her daughter disappear through the operating room doors with Jesus at her side, holding her hand. The surgery was successful, and today Savannah is a bright, articulate, happy toddler with a twinkle in her eye. It is almost as though she knows a secret and remembers hearing Mercy's voice, "Little girl, get up."

Sharing Our Hearts

Discussion Starters

Reflect on the following thoughts we will discuss together. Take particular note of those that strike a chord with you and add notes in the margin about them.

1. Have you been through a time of great distress and chose to trust God?

   _____

   _____

   _____

2. Can you name some of the things you have done in reaching out to another who is grieving? Add to this list of ideas of what others have done.

   ❑ sent cards

   ❑ telephoned on a regular basis

   ❑ gave a hug or a touch

   ❑ spent time listening over a cup of coffee or on a walk

   ❑ shared a book, poem, or Scripture verse

   ❑ was present as a supporter, without having to do or say anything

   ❑ provided a home-cooked meal or a plate of cookies

   ❑ picked up groceries or children

   ❑ ran errands

   ❑ prayed for and with her

   ❑ cried with her

❑ other: _____

_____

_____

_____

3. How do hard times bring you to the feet of Jesus and to a richer trust in God? Add your thoughts to what others have said.

- "I trust Him more because I don't know who else to trust."

- "I am sad to say that I did not think about God much at all before this tragedy."

- "When I got over being mad at God, I realized He was not mad at me for being mad. I saw that He actually was sad and wept with me in my pain and disappointment."

- "Everybody falls short of perfect love and will eventually leave me. God is the only perfect Person I know and He won't leave me. That makes me love Him more."

- "No one can be with me twenty-four hours a day to help me in my grief and loneliness. Only God can. And He is! When a friend calls me, I know God sent them to comfort me at that moment."

- "The Bible was just a book before this happened. Now I hear God talking to me personally in the verses."

❑ other: _____

_____

_____

_____

_____

_____

4. The position of kneeling in prayer is within our power to choose every day, and it pleases God. What inhibits your prayer life?

- ❏ It's hard work.
- ❏ It hurts my pride and hurts my knees.
- ❏ I'm uncomfortable with the silence.
- ❏ I fall asleep.
- ❏ I can't see the One I'm praying to.
- ❏ I don't see instant results.
- ❏ other: _____
  _____
  _____
  _____

5. How can you be a friend others can trust?

- ❏ be real
- ❏ be loving
- ❏ be available
- ❏ get a life–His life
- ❏ be ready to listen and maintain confidence
- ❏ other: _____
  _____
  _____
  _____
  _____
  _____

A Change of Heart

Lesson Summary and Application

One main thought I have gleaned from the lesson:

_____

_____

_____

_____

One application of this lesson to my life: With God's help . . .

❏ I will stop doubting and start trusting for _____

_____

_____

❏ I will seek to become a more trustworthy friend.

❏ I will choose the position of kneeling in prayer more often.

❏ other: _____

_____

_____

Walk the Word

❏ Observe someone who is trusting an authority such as a teacher, police officer, or boss. Listen to the words being said and watch the actions of the individuals.

❏ Notice how you can trust people for some things, but not for everything.

❏ Make someone the object of your love by seeking to encourage them.

Notes

Hearing His Heart

The following verses on this week's topic, "A Friend Trusts,"
are given for deepening your love for the Lord and for
others. Space is provided after each verse for you to record
your thoughts.

WEEK 1

Monday

Psalm 13:5

"But I trust in your _____ ."

_____

_____

_____

Tuesday

Proverbs 3:5

*"Trust in _____ with all your heart and lean not
on your own understanding."*

_____

_____

_____

Wednesday

Exodus 14:31

*"And when the Israelites saw the great power the LORD displayed
against the Egyptians, the people _____
and _____ and in Moses his
servant."*

_____

_____

_____

Thursday

Isaiah 50:10

"Let him who walks in the dark, _____ ,
trust in the _____ and rely on
his God."

_____

_____

_____

Friday

Psalm 56:4

"In God _____ ; I will not be afraid."

_____

_____

_____

WEEK 2

Monday

1 Corinthians 13:6-7

"Love does not delight in evil but _____ .
It always protects, _____ , always hopes,
always perseveres."

_____

_____

_____

Tuesday

1 Peter 2:6

"… the one who _____ will never be
put to shame."

_____
_____
_____

Wednesday

1 Chronicles 5:20
" ... *He answered their prayers, because* _____
in Him."

_____
_____
_____

Thursday

John 14:1
"*Do not let your hearts be troubled.* _____ ;
trust also in me."

_____
_____
_____

Friday

Proverbs 28:25
"*A greedy man* _____ ,
but he who _____ *will prosper.*"

_____
_____
_____

Notes

CHAPTER 4

Mary and Martha

A Friend Listens and Serves

"No one can develop freely in this world and find a full life without feeling understood by at least one person. Misunderstood, he loses his self-confidence, he loses his faith in life or even in God. It is impossible to overemphasize the immense need men have to be really listened to, to be taken seriously, to be understood."

—Paul Tournier

Scripture Reading: Luke 10:38-42

What factors are important in entertaining guests? What do our friends really need or want when they come into our homes? A four-course meal? A spotless house? A listening ear? Perhaps all of the above, but maybe something else as well. A look at this passage will enable us to discern what is needed most and to learn how to give it so that others will enjoy visiting our homes.

 certain guest has been invited to the home of Mary and Martha, but this is not just any guest. This is their Friend, Jesus, who has become of late an important personage in the community. Therefore, it is necessary that preparations be carried out meticulously. Mary and Martha are both aware of their guest's stature, but it appears that only Martha is dedicated to staying on task—to the point of anxiety and exhaustion—as she drives herself to attend lovingly to every detail of an impressive meal for Him.

As though in final insult to her already irritated sister, Mary has the audacity to sit down when the Guest arrives. Martha observes incredulously that Mary is acting like a guest herself. As Martha continues to seethe in the face of this totally unacceptable behavior, the volcano of resentment inside her begins to boil over. Finally, she can hold it in no longer and blurts out to their Honored Guest, who seems pleased to be talking with someone who is willing to offer Him her undivided attention, *"Lord, don't you care that my sister has left me to do the work by myself? Tell her to help me"* (Luke 10:40).

Jesus has a reputation for caring, and Martha, perhaps inadvertently, has chosen the appropriate phrase for this confrontational moment. The air feels thick as Jesus, the Guest, is asked to take sides. It is not the first time He has been placed in this position.

Just a chapter earlier, He was asked by his disciples to identify who among them was the greatest (Luke 9:46). This seems to be a common theme among His friends. Many want to be His favorite in order to get what they want, while ignoring what He wants.

In the face of this direct challenge, Jesus can no longer ignore the incessant activity of this woman running back and forth, banging pottery and pans and muttering under her breath. He interrupts His dialogue with Mary and His initial unexpected silence gains the needed full attention from Martha.

The Guest has something to say that He does not want Martha to miss. To make certain that she hears it, He calls her by name—twice. This is the only recorded instance in the Gospels in which Jesus repeats a woman's name when addressing her. Martha may have been expecting the name *Mary* to come out of His mouth in a gentle rebuke to her negligent sister. Instead, she hears her own name spoken with a curious combination of tenderness and rebuke: *"Martha, Martha"* (Luke 10:41). And what follows is a message for all women that penetrates to the core of our beings: *"You are worried and upset about many things."*

Oh, are we ever! How we women tend to excel at worrying. Then Jesus continues, choosing His words carefully: *"But only one thing is needed. Mary has chosen what is better, and it will not be taken away from her"* (Luke 10:41). Jesus does address Mary, but not in the way Martha had expected. He *commends* Mary, and that makes absolutely no sense to task-oriented Martha.

Without a heart change, these words will never make sense. Jesus is not about ensuring equal rights but about entering hearts. He is not about choosing sides, but about changing priorities. He is not about selecting a favorite, but about satisfying a thirsty heart. He is not about what will impress our guests, but about what will impact them. For that matter, what is it that will impact them?

The Friend spells this out for Martha plainly and simply. Listen again, and don't allow the brevity of the message to deceive you into thinking it is unimportant. These words are a critical key for living life as God intended: *"Mary has chosen what is better and it will not be taken away from her."*

Relationship with God is always the better choice. It is a choice for the eternal, and it never will be snatched away. Immediately beneath it in priority are relationships with other people. People are eternal, while things are temporary—never the other way around. Things are to be used to love people, and not people used because we love things. "Things," whether they be activities or tangible objects, must never come between God, or other people, and ourselves.

Oh, God knows there are a lot of good and worthwhile "things." Food preparation, especially as a gesture of love, is a commendable activity. A comfortable and spotless house and well-manicured lawn are pleasant things to enjoy. A beautifully set table is admirable. But if we become upset with others, or place things higher in priority than enjoying a relationship with our friends, then our priorities have become skewed.

When our anxiety pollutes a peaceful atmosphere, then whatever activity we are engaged in is not the better thing. It is, in fact, not even good. It is unwelcome, undesirable, and unattractive. When a hostess cannot spare the time to sit down with her guest, demonstrating that she is honored by the friend's presence, conversation, and friendship, she has missed the point of entertaining. The same holds true for planning for Women's Ministry banquets or preparing meals for our families. How often we sacrifice what is eternal on a cheap altar of temporary busyness, and in the process forfeit the love and grace that could have been ours.

Somehow Mary has understood this. She has *"sat at the Lord's feet, listening to what He said"* (Luke 10:39). First and foremost, she has listened. Friends do. Close friends listen closely. In listening closely, Mary opens herself up to learn. She understands Jesus in ways few do as He shares what is on His heart. She may not like everything she has been hearing (some things may have to do with His future suffering), but she does not react. She responds. Just think of it: The whole world has been told about her selfless expression of love simply because she took the time to listen and respond.

Mary chooses the better thing—to offer her Guest her undivided attention. She rightly identifies her most precious possession as an open and listening heart. In those few moments she spends seated at Jesus' feet, she is given not only an eternal awareness but a passion for His words that will later result in a unique and unforgettable act of worship. An undying ember of love has been kindled in Mary's heart. She knows that she is loved and she desires to reciprocate that love. How can she do so?

While Mary listens, Martha serves. Serving is very important. It is more than just commendable. Jesus said, "Whoever wants to become great among you must be your servant" (Matthew 20:26). He Himself took "the very nature of a servant" (Philippians 2:7). Oh, how needed and necessary and in short supply, it seems, good servants are. But serving is not all we need to do any more than listening is all we need to do. Both are necessary. There must be a balance.

To serve without listening to God causes us to be easily upset and critical of others. To listen to God without serving causes us to be unproductive, irresponsible, and stunted in our spiritual growth. Both are equally needed but one is *better*. Listening first and foremost to the heart of Jesus results in a deeper love relationship with Him. We capture eternity's values and they soak into our hearts, sensitizing us to His will for our lives. Listening to others results in deeper love relationships with them. And because of our relationship with Christ, we pass along those eternal values, thus enriching others' hearts and serving them effectively—but the relationships will last long after the serving has ceased.

Certainly people enjoy food and atmosphere when they come into our homes. Martha understood that. But Mary understood that they need something more—our love exemplified by our presence. The food and beauty must be presented on a platter of grace, or what's the point? Martha did demonstrate her love and admiration for Jesus by opening her home and serving Him. That was commendable, but it was not lasting because, although she was giving with the one hand, she was taking with the other through her worry and frustration. Mary, by contrast, was making memories—beautiful lasting memories—as she connected in her heart to Jesus. She was also making plans. Those plans were about to cost her dearly.

A Modern Day Lesson:
Learning to Listen

In order to live well, we must listen well. And in listening well, we will respond well and not resist truth. How can you listen well and then respond appropriately? The comparisons below show that a humble attitude builds bridges, while a proud attitude erects walls.

Bridge Builders humble attitude seen in:	Wall Erectors proud attitude seen in:
• showing acceptance	• being judgmental or condemning
• affirming people	• being critical of people and their beliefs
• being teachable	• being resistant
• focusing on coming alongside people	• focusing on fixing people
• knowing I am different, not better than others	• acting as though I am better and more special to God
• having empathy to find common ground	• looking at how different and hopeless others are
• admitting I don't have a monopoly on truth	• always having an answer for everything
• praying to the One who listens best	• doubting that God listens or cares
• being open-minded	• being closed-minded

Sharing Our Hearts

Discussion Starters

Reflect on the following thoughts we will discuss together. Take particular note of those that strike a chord with you and add notes in the margin about them.

1. Needs are as varied as people are. But one need is basic. People need to feel that they are important, not just in general, but to us personally. What do you do to make others feel important?

   ❏ Call them by name.

   ❏ Invite them over to my house.

   ❏ Send them a card or e-mail.

   ❏ Compliment them.

   ❏ Go out of my way to greet them.

   ❏ Listen to them, maintaining eye contact.

   ❏ Set aside time to be with them.

   ❏ Ask them about themselves.

   ❏ other: _____

   _____

   _____

   _____

   _____

2. How can you be a better friend so that others will enjoy coming to your home?

   ❏ Greet them warmly at the door.

   ❏ Share from my heart an encouraging word.

❏ Speak kindly to them.

❏ Pray with them.

❏ Fuss over them a little, being careful not to overdo it.

❏ other: _____

_____

_____

3. When you have felt as though you were getting "the short end of the stick," what has been your response?

❏ to quit

❏ to complain

❏ to look for another job or friend

❏ to eat chocolate

❏ to love faithfully

❏ to pray for a changed attitude

❏ other: _____

_____

_____

_____

4. What are some of the benefits when you "sit at His feet" through prayer and study?

❏ knowing and feeling I am

• valued and important
• focused on a truly important purpose
• accepted and forgiven
• protected and provided for
• listened to, as well as receptive to His voice

- ❏ a peaceful resignation that "what doesn't get done doesn't matter"
- ❏ strength from His presence and His words
- ❏ a bigger view of life and a smaller view of things
- ❏ other: _____

  _____

  _____

  _____

  _____

  _____

5. What distractions prevent you from enjoying friendship with God and with others?

- ❏ my hectic schedule
- ❏ my desire for independence
- ❏ my fear of trusting
- ❏ my selfishness
- ❏ my indifference
- ❏ my desire to make and spend money
- ❏ other: _____

  _____

  _____

  _____

  _____

  _____

  _____

  _____

A Change of Heart

Lesson Summary and Application

One main thought I have gleaned from the lesson:

_____

_____

_____

_____

One application of this lesson to my life: With God's help . . .

❏ I will be a better listener to _____

_____

❏ I will get a grip on my attitude and will serve others graciously.

❏ I will choose a balance between listening and serving.

❏ other: _____

_____

_____

_____

Walk the Word

❏ Hold your tongue and listen to someone you normally don't listen to.

❏ Draw closer to God and people by listening intently.

❏ Observe the attitude of someone whose job it is to serve customers, such as a sales clerk, a waitress, or a checker. Speak to this person and watch his or her response.

Notes

Hearing His Heart

The following verses on this week's topic, "A Friend Listens and Serves," are given for deepening your love for the Lord and for others. Space is provided after each verse for you to record your thoughts.

Monday

James 1:19-21

"My dear brothers, take note of this: Everyone should be quick to _____ , slow to speak and slow to become angry, for man's anger does not bring about the righteous life that God desires. Therefore, get rid of all moral filth and the evil that is so prevalent and humbly accept the word planted in you, which can save you."

_____

_____

_____

Tuesday

1 Samuel 12:24

"Be sure to fear the LORD and _____ him faithfully with all your heart; consider what great things He has done for you."

_____

_____

_____

Wednesday

Proverbs 18:13

"He who answers before listening—that is his folly and _____."

_____

_____

_____

Thursday

Joshua 22:5

*"Be very careful to keep the commandment and the law that Moses the servant of the LORD gave you: to love the LORD your God, to walk in all His ways, to _____ ,
to hold fast to Him and to serve Him with _____
_____."*

_____

_____

_____

Friday

Deuteronomy 30:19-20

"Now choose life, so that you and your children may live and that you may love the LORD your God, _____ to His voice and hold fast to Him. For the LORD is _____ and He will give you many years in the land he swore to give your fathers, Abraham, Isaac and Jacob."

_____

_____

_____

WEEK 2

Monday

Ephesians 6:7-8

*" _____ wholeheartedly, as if you were _____
the LORD, not men, because you know that the LORD will reward everyone for whatever good he does, whether he is slave or free."*

_____

_____

_____

Tuesday

1 Peter 4:10

"Each one should use whatever gift he has received to _____ others, faithfully administering God's grace in its various forms."

_____

_____

_____

Wednesday

John 12:26

"Whoever _____ must follow me; and where I am, my servant also will be."

_____

_____

_____

Thursday

Mark 10:45

"Even the Son of Man did not come to be served, but to _____ , and to give His life a ransom for many."

_____

_____

_____

Friday

Ecclesiastes 5:1

"Guard your steps when you go to the house of God. Go near to _____ rather than to offer the sacrifice of fools, who do not know that they do wrong."

_____

_____

_____

CHAPTER **5**

Mary, Mother of the Child Jesus

A Friend Is Honest

"No one could have prepared me for this.
Nothing I had read or seen
Could describe the exquisite joy of my soul.
'I'm a mother!' Me! Oh, heart, be still.
Who is this sweet, pink face—so fresh from heaven—
Peeking out from beneath her blanket cocoon?
Oh, God, you have such faith and trust in me.
Please stay close and whisper in my ear
The things I need to know.
I want to do my best."

—Kathy Erickson

Scripture Reading: Luke 1 and 2

Have you ever thought about what it would be like to live in the household of a perfect child? Or for that matter, to be His mother? What would she need to be like to handle Him? Only one woman has ever been in that position, and she did not talk a lot about it. But what the authors of the Gospels do record of her is significant and speaks to us about one outstanding quality that is essential in having a healthy, loving relationship with anyone.

he Gospel writers give us a unique portrait of this woman's life over a thirty-four-year span. We see her from her engagement as a young teenager of fifteen or sixteen, so historians say, to a mid-lifer of forty-eight or forty-nine. More biblical commentary is devoted to her and to her life than to that of any other New Testament woman. That alone makes us take note of her biography. But a second and infinitely more important reason that she is significant has to do not with Mary herself but with who she is related to. Mary is, incredible as it may seem, the mother of Jesus. As *mother* of the Son of God, she has been given by God an exclusive place in time and history— a position such as no other has been or ever again will be given.

Mary is her name, and mothering is her calling. In Luke 1 this modest teenaged girl embarks on her mission and calling to be a faithful, nurturing, sacrificial mom. To do this she will have to demonstrate unusual courage, patience, perseverance in suffering, and commitment—along with one other essential character quality: *honesty*.

As the first scene opens (Luke 1:26), the angel Gabriel appears to Mary to pass along a message directly from God. Seeing an angel would no doubt instill terror in any woman's heart. Mary is no exception. In addition, this is no "ordinary" angel. This is the one and only Gabriel, who makes his appearance only on the rarest of occasions. Mary may have recalled from her schooling at Nazareth Elementary that Gabriel had shown up for Daniel. What he had to say to him on that occasion troubled Daniel for weeks and puzzled mankind for centuries. Most recently, he has appeared to Mary's relative Zechariah, and he has been unable to speak ever since. To say that she is *"greatly troubled"* (Luke1:29) is to put it mildly.

Nevertheless, Mary innately senses how *not* to respond to an angel's visit. One is not to question him to certify that he is for real. Instead, the one so favored is to receive the message with open mind and heart, neither resisting nor doubting God's Word.

What the trembling but receptive young woman hears Gabriel say is beyond her wildest imagination. For centuries every woman in Israel has dreamed about hearing words similar to these: *"Do not be afraid, Mary, you have found favor with God. You will be with child and give birth to a son, and you are to give him the name Jesus. He will be great and will be called the Son of the Most High"* (Luke 1:31). Mary has been singled out from among all the women of history to be mother of the long-awaited Messiah.

There is, however, one "minor" problem. Mary is neither ignorant nor naïve. She knows the facts. She is not married, so someone will need to convincingly inform her fiancé, Joseph, about the validity of all of this. This is after all to be a *super*natural birth, because this Life and mission will be *extra*ordinary. No man could impregnate Mary with such a child—in a bed, lab or test tube.

Then Gabriel explains the method, which mysteriously involves both the Holy Spirit and power, adding the assurance that *"nothing is impossible with God"* (Luke 1:37). And that is the end of the discussion. Nothing more needs to be said—only obedient actions are required. Mary's response is admirable. She graciously receives this incredible message, expressing humbly, *"I am the Lord's servant; may it be to me as you have said"* (Luke 1:38).

True to Gabriel's word, Jesus is conceived as the Holy Spirit comes upon Mary in a unique way. This has to be a glorious moment for her, and for God. But the joy of the conception seems short-lived because her pregnancy now causes her public humiliation and private rejection by her fiancé, Joseph, who has as yet received no divine revelation and sees no alternative but to divorce her (engagements in her day are in some sense the equivalent of marriages).

At the appropriate moment, however, God again steps into the scene by sending an angel to speak to Joseph in a dream (Matthew 1:20). This confirmation gives Mary needed affirmation, protection, and support. However, neither God nor any angel appears to the multitude of people around her, so Mary continues to bear the lifelong stigma of an out-of-wedlock pregnancy. The sword that will pierce to the depths of her heart has now begun its descent into her soul and will climax its relentless assault when her beloved son is executed on a cross.

Some thirteen years later we see another snapshot of Mary's life as a twenty-eight-year-old mom who is celebrating and feasting with her family and friends (Luke 2:41). She and Joseph by this time have had four other sons, James, Joseph, Simon, and Judas as well as some daughters (Matthew 13:55). This particular visit to Jerusalem is bittersweet. On the one hand, it has been marvelous to be with relatives and friends in the faith, rejoicing in the celebration of Passover. But on the other, this distraught mother is now a full day into her journey home, in the company of many fellow travelers, and has discovered that she cannot find her twelve-year-old son, Jesus. Not a soul in the company, including his fun-loving pack of adolescent buddies, has seen Him since yesterday's departure from Jerusalem.

Now any normal mother of a normal child would be upset. But this is an extraordinary child, and the tension must be even greater because it involves someone so chosen who has been entrusted to her care. How is she ever going to explain this apparent mishap to her family and friends, to the prophets, to the people of Israel or to God Himself?

You can imagine her joy and relief, then, when after an agonizing three-day search she does indeed locate her precious child. Where has He been? Why, of all places, in the temple, His Father's house. And can you imagine what He is doing? He is listening, discoursing, and asking penetrating and important questions, to the amazement of all in attendance.

Mary then speaks the first words to her son that are recorded in Scripture. Here we have a major clue as to the essential quality for an imperfect mother raising the perfect Son. Upon first reading, we wish her words had been different. You know, sweeter, more empathetic, wiser. Had she known ahead of time that they were going to be recorded for all posterity, she might have spoken something charming, quotable, profound. But that wouldn't have been Mary. Here we have a woman who is real with her emotions and perspective. That's the point. *She is honest in her feelings towards her son.* She is neither pretending nor holding back.

And if you cannot be honest and real in front of Jesus, who can you be honest with?

So Mary speaks what is on her mind. *"Son, why have you treated us like this? Your father and I have been anxiously searching for you"* (Luke 2:48). Translated, this means that she has been doing what so many moms do so well. She's been worrying. And she scolds him. Part of the reason for her anxiety is that she does not understand her son (Luke 2:50). She, who has borne this amazing child, lived with Him, nurtured Him, and guided Him, still does not know or comprehend Him completely. Then young Jesus wisely replies to her in the form of two questions, a method He will use often in His later teaching: *"Why were you searching for me? Didn't you know I had to be in my Father's house?"* (Luke 2:49).

Mary apparently says nothing. That is probably wise. What does one say in the presence of God when one has just shown how human she is once again, for the thousandth time? Whether or not she responds will not affect Jesus' actions as they relate to His parents. He continues loving them and being obedient (Luke 2:50), and Mary continues treasuring this wonderful puzzle of challenges and joys, just like any normal mom would do. She recognizes that her son's world has expanded. He is making it clear that there is another house and family that He needs to attend to. She will have Him still for eighteen more years (longer, certainly, than most of us continue to nurture our children in the nest!) and then He will embark on His brief but history-changing mission. How is she going to handle that? Near the end of that time what quality besides honesty will see her through as Jesus' mom and friend?

A Modern Day Story
Julie: An Honest Wife

I rejoiced with Julie who told me, "It was four years ago on Valentine's Day that my husband gave me a new wedding ring and proclaimed that he now loved me again as a wife. God has blessed our obedience. As I look at our marriage and into the beautiful faces of our two little children, I am constantly reminded of how awesome our God is. And as I look over the past years, there have been times I have walked in obedience to God, and times when I have turned away from God in my human anger. But He has been patient and faithful. As I told my pastor the day after John asked me for the divorce, 'No matter what happens, I am thankful to God that through this situation I have experienced God in a way that I would not trade for anything.' I no longer doubt my salvation!"

Whenever my path crosses with Julie's, I am reminded of a woman who is sincere in her desire to be the wife and mom God created her to be. I always leave encouraged because I know God's heart is open toward her because her heart is open toward Him.

Sharing Our Hearts

Discussion Starters

Reflect on the following thoughts we will discuss together. Take particular note of those that strike a chord with you and add notes in the margin about them.

1. What kind of advice did your mother give you?

_____

_____

_____

_____

_____

2. Being honest looks different for each person. Name some ways that you are honest before God.

   ❏ I don't try to be perfect.

   ❏ I give myself permission to feel either joy or grief.

   ❏ I accept loss and disappointment as His appointments.

   ❏ When I am wrong, I say that I am sorry.

   ❏ other: _____

   _____

   _____

   _____

   _____

3. What kinds of miracles does God perform in your life today?

   ❏ He has given me a new heart of tenderness toward Himself and others.

❑ He has rearranged my value system so that I think about others and not only about myself.

❑ He has healed me from _____

❑ He has provided all I need for today.

❑ He has done what people say is impossible to do.

❑ He has forgiven me and given me a second chance.

❑ other: _____

_____

_____

_____

_____

_____

_____

_____

4. Why is it important to be honest in a friendship?

❑ It builds trust.

❑ It knits hearts together.

❑ It eliminates confusion.

❑ It is the only way to come to God, our greatest Friend.

❑ It's the key to greater communication and intimacy.

❑ It relieves guilt.

❑ other: _____

_____

_____

_____

_____

A Change of Heart

Lesson Summary and Application

One main thought I have gleaned from the lesson:

_____

_____

_____

_____

One application of this lesson to my life: With God's help . . .

- ❏ I will attempt to be less of a perfectionist and more authentic with others.

- ❏ I will speak the honest truth in a loving way.

- ❏ When I am at odds with someone else, I will be the first to apologize and own up to my part of the wrongdoing.

- ❏ other: _____

    _____

    _____

Walk the Word

- ❏ Take note of ways in which the newspaper and TV can make people look better than they really are.

- ❏ Watch the reactions of someone who is a good judge of character.

- ❏ Observe a child and notice how "real" he or she is.

Notes

_____

_____

_____

_____

_____

_____

_____

_____

Out of the Mouths of Babes

A friend told me a story of a mother and her three-year-old daughter who were watching TV. A news clip came on about a famous person who had died. The child's immediate reaction was, "Is he going to heaven?" Her mom explained that he would go to heaven if he had asked Jesus to be his Savior. The child proceeded to ask the question about every family member she could think of. Not be left out, she added, "You know what, Mom? I talked to Jesus on the phone the other day and I asked Him to come into my heart."

"That's great," the mom said, "but how did you know His number?"

Her reply was simple, but profound. "He called *me*."

That in a nutshell is the difference between Christianity and religion. Christianity is God reaching out to man and religion is man doing everything he can to reach out to God.

—As told by Lolie Pineda

Hearing His Heart

The following verses on this week's topic, "A Friend Is Honest," are given for deepening your love for the Lord and for others. Space is provided after each verse for you to record your thoughts.

WEEK 1

Monday

John 4:24

"God is spirit, and His worshipers must worship in spirit and in _____ ."

_____

_____

_____

Tuesday

Proverbs 16:13

"Kings take pleasure in _____ ; they value a man who speaks the truth."

_____

_____

_____

Wednesday

Ephesians 4:15

"Speaking the _____ , we will in all things grow up into Him who is the Head, that is, Christ."

_____

_____

_____

Thursday

Psalm 51:6

"Surely you desire _____ in the inner parts; you teach me wisdom in the inmost place."

_____

_____

_____

Friday

1 John 1:8

"If we claim to be without _____ , we deceive ourselves and the _____ is not in us."

_____

_____

_____

WEEK 2

Monday

Jeremiah 5:1

"'Go up and down the streets of Jerusalem, look around and consider, search through her squares. If you can find but one person who _____ , I will forgive this city.'"

_____

_____

_____

Tuesday

Psalm 15:1-2

"LORD, who may dwell in your sanctuary? Who may live on your holy hill? He whose walk is blameless and who does what is righteous, who speaks the _____ from his heart."

_____

_____

_____

Wednesday

1 Corinthians 5:8

"Let us keep the Festival, not with the old yeast, the yeast of malice and wickedness, but with bread without yeast, the bread of _____ ."

_____

_____

_____

Thursday

Proverbs 12:17-20,22

"A truthful witness gives honest testimony, but a false witness tells lies. Reckless words pierce like a sword, but the tongue of the wise brings healing. Truthful lips endure forever, but a lying tongue lasts only a moment. There is deceit in the hearts of those who plot evil, but joy for those who promote peace.... The LORD detests lying lips, but He delights in men who are _____ ."

_____

_____

_____

Friday

Zechariah 8:16

"Speak the _____ to each other, and render true and sound judgment in your courts."

_____

_____

_____

Mary, Mother of the Man Jesus

A Friend Is Accepting

He Maketh No Mistake

*M*y Father's way may twist and turn,
My heart may throb and ache;
But in my soul I'm glad I know
He maketh no mistake.

My cherished plans may go astray,
My hope may fade away,
But still I'll trust my Lord to lead,
For He doth know the way.

Tho' night be dark and it may seem
That day will never break;
I'll pin my faith, my all on Him,
He maketh no mistake.

There's so much now I cannot see,
My eyesight's far too dim;
But come what may, I'll simply trust
And leave it all to Him.

For by and by the mist will lift
And plain it all He'll make.
Through all the way, tho' dark to me
He made not one mistake.

—A.M. Overton

Scripture Reading: John 2:1-5,
Mark 3:20-21 and John 19:25-27

We have seen that an essential quality of a successful mother is honesty with regard to her feelings and perspective. That same quality is vital for a friendship to be fully enjoyed and treasured. Mary, Jesus' mother, has modeled that wonderfully. Now she has entered a new passage in life. What is she learning, and what personal quality is indispensable for a mid-lifer whose oldest son is leaving the nest?

ighteen years have passed and the Gospel writers provide us with two new snapshots of an older, more mature Mother Mary at about the age of forty-six. One picture is in John 2:1 and the other is in Mark 3:31. Her Son is ready to embark on His three-and-one-half-year mission of preaching, teaching, and performing miracles. It is believed that Mary has been widowed, since there is no mention that Joseph is still with her.

Jesus and His mother are attending a wedding where Jesus is about to perform His first miracle. In this passage Mary, the seasoned woman of experience, speaks her last recorded words in Scripture, and these words are definitely worth noting. She has lived with Jesus longer than anyone else has, so her observation about the Son of God is surely accurate and important. Any advice she has to offer will be invaluable, coming, as it does, from the perspective of daily contact for the past three decades with a pair of heavenly antennae.

The wedding reception is in full swing. It is a joyful occasion, except for one glitch: Someone has miscalculated how much wine would be needed, and the hosts have run out. This is not a life-or-death situation, but it is a definite social etiquette issue that needs immediate, behind-the-scenes attention. Mary notices the dilemma of her friends and informs Jesus of it, presumably not for the sake of idle conversation but because she knows that her

Son has the ability to solve the problem. Jesus' reply is intriguing: *"Dear woman, why do you involve me? My time has not yet come"* (John 2:4). Now Mary knows her extraordinary Son well enough to realize He is not flatly declining to help. The fact is that it is God's nature to help. So her final words in Scripture, though brief, carry meaning and reveal wisdom far beyond the surface statement. She simply directs the servants: *"Do whatever He tells you to do"* (John 2:5). They oblige, and miraculously the water is transformed into the finest wine. Mary's down-to-earth words are still today the best possible advice for whatever problem, tiny or titanic, that any of us may face.

Jesus continues His public ministry, and at another point His mother and brothers appear on the scene (Mark 3:31). They desire to see Him and dispatch someone into the house to give Him the message. Jesus' response most likely surprises them. They probably expect VIP treatment, but Jesus calmly reminds them, by means of a message, of His "other" family. Characteristically, the Lord asks a provocative question: *"Who are my mother and my brothers?"* (Mark 3:33). Gazing about at those seated in a circle around Him, He declares with an expansive gesture, *"Here are my mother and my brothers! Whoever does God's will is my brother and sister and mother."*

Although Jesus is not rude to His mother, He is definitely cutting the apron strings. She needs to accept the reality that her active role as full-time mother has come to an end. Others have entered His heart, and they will fill spaces that were once reserved especially for her. Oh, Mary will still have a special place, but the situation will be forever different from what it has been before.

And so Mary lives out the rest of her days, at least insofar as the

Scripture narrative is concerned, in the shadows. We hear about her only three times more. The first is the time she and the children come again on a private mission to "rescue" Jesus on account of His "insanity" (Mark 3:20-21). While we cannot help but marvel at her lack of understanding in this instance, we are reminded once again of her honesty in expressing her feelings and opinions.

The second appearance undoubtedly represents the darkest moment of Mary's life, as we observe her standing, distraught, beneath the cross (John 19:25), viewing her precious Son alive for the last time. Bleeding and torn, Jesus hangs in gory disgrace in a position ordinarily reserved for a condemned criminal. But it soon becomes apparent that Jesus has not forgotten the earthly mother who has given Him birth and raised Him lovingly, all the while aware of His unique status as a precious trust from God. Despite His agony and physical depletion, He musters the strength to speak lovingly to His mother, tenderly addressing her overwhelming need and pain.

Just as Mary had heard His first baby cry, so now she is present to hear His dying words and His final, agonizing cry. She, who had marveled privately at the joy of His entry into the world, now groans with Him in utter grief and excruciating pain as He departs.

Before Jesus' death, a sword pierces His side, and the emotional sword that had already pierced Mary some thirty-four years earlier thrusts itself deeply into her already bleeding mother-heart. She has been His confidante and faithful friend, and He hers. She has not always understood Him, but she has loved Him with a mother's complete abandon and has accepted the inevitable path of suffering from the manger to the grave. Mary has excelled in loving well and sacrificially. She and Son are in this way very much alike.

Mary takes the stage one last time forty days later, when she gathers with other believers in the Upper Room waiting for the promised Holy Spirit. Although she is apparently silent (at least none of her words are recorded), she is not absent. Her presence here is significant. The same Holy Spirit who had come upon her as a young teenager was about to be poured out upon a multitude. Many would now be empowered to become spiritual mothers, brothers, sisters, and fathers, doing the will of God to bring forth life and to nurture children in His kingdom.

Mary had modeled well what it looked like to say yes to the Spirit—to be open-minded and open-hearted. She had accepted God's perfect, though inexplicable, will for her life even during those times when she was fearful, ashamed, lacking in understanding, struggling to let go, or emotionally hemorrhaging. Mary's exemplary life still demonstrates for us today that a serene trust and acceptance of God's plans enable any of us to live life exactly as God has intended.

When life hurts and the jagged pieces fail to fall into place no matter how hard we try, we can find comfort in God's presence, as well as the strength we need to enable us to accept the cup He has for us to drink. We can do that well only when we, like Mary, realize that the story is not about us, but about Him and His unconditional love for us. In receiving Him and listening to Him well through loving obedience to His words, we will find our own special places in His forever family of faith. And yes, we will even begin to look like Him!

A Modern Day Story
Beth: A Widow Who Is Accepting

"Now that I have survived that horrible morning of two years ago, I realize that some of the silly things I had found to worry about are truly insignificant compared to watching the one you love the most die before your eyes. I am convinced that if God brought me through this, there is nothing, absolutely nothing, He can't bring me through. Impossible? Oh, yes, impossible for me, but by His great love and grace it's possible. Am I broken-hearted? Absolutely! Am I lonely? Most certainly! Do I long for what I had? Oh, yes. Oh, yes, I long. Big mountains still need to be moved in my life, but God promises if I have faith even as small as a mustard seed, He'll move the mountains.

"As God continues showing me the impossibilities becoming possible, I am learning that I cannot only live a joyous life for Him, but He tugs at my heart-strings to step out for Him. I believe He is inviting me to use my pain and sorrow to reach out to others. Through prayer, circumstances, and a tugging at my heart, I can hear Him say, 'Come on, Beth, I know it's tough. But I am not through with you yet. There's work to be done, and I want to use you and your suffering. Look, just look, at the incredible pain and suffering out there. Other widows grieve. What of the ones who have lost a child? Look at those who live in the emptiness of an unhappy marriage, or those who long for the love of a companion. You know how that feels. So many hurts, so much guilt. Those who carry the burden of guilt from infidelity or abortion. You know how brokenness and pain feels. Come reach out to them with me!'"

Beth always encourages me. No one ever remains a stranger for very long in her presence. Her warm and inviting ways draw others in, her hospitality is always overflowing, and her heart is excited and open to whatever new thing God brings into her life.

Sharing Our Hearts

Discussion Starters

1. What road have you traveled that has not been easy?

_____

_____

_____

_____

2. When others do not meet your expectations, how do you respond?

   ❏ I tell them so.

   ❏ I withdraw and sulk.

   ❏ I withdraw and pray.

   ❏ I go shopping.

   ❏ I overeat.

   ❏ I refuse to think about it.

   ❏ I watch TV.

   ❏ I accept it.

   ❏ other: _____

   _____

   _____

   _____

   _____

   _____

   _____

   _____

   _____

3. Earthly family is important. But a spiritual family of faith is in some sense even more important. If you really believe that, how can you express it?

❏ by being an active participant in my church community

❏ by giving of myself and my talents to love those in the church

❏ by being available to call or receive a call from a friend

❏ by not expecting others to fill a need that I am able to fill

❏ by sharing my earthly family with others

❏ other: _____

_____

_____

_____

_____

4. It is natural to worry and to be afraid. It is "super"-natural to bring our worries to God and face our fears through prayer, so that peace and courage can fill our hearts. What are some of your worries and fears?

❏ my children's futures

❏ violence (being robbed, raped, or attacked)

❏ not having enough money

❏ being unable to retire

❏ never marrying

❏ marrying the wrong man

❏ being unable to have children

❏ losing my health

❏ other: _____

_____

_____

5. Many women feel inferior to Mary. Anyone who does God's will in the areas of trusting Him and loving others is just as important to God as Mary was—and is considered to be a part of His family (Mark 3:33). What is your response to that knowledge?

❏ I doubt that it is true.

❏ I am surprised and in awe that it could possibly be so.

❏ I am grateful that He would be so gracious to me.

❏ I want to trust as I seek to do His will, like Mary did.

❏ other: _____

_____

_____

_____

_____

Anyone who does God's will in the areas of trusting Him and loving others can be a Mary. Does this sound like a description of your character? If you can identify in yourself even an element of resemblance to Mary, draw a timeline of your life, filling in some of these significant events that exemplify this spirit. List those times when it was hard to trust God or to be an accepting family member or friend.

_____
_____
_____
_____
_____
_____
_____
_____
_____
_____
_____
_____
_____
_____
_____
_____
_____
_____
_____
_____

A Change of Heart

Lesson Summary and Application

One main thought I have gleaned from the lesson:

_____
_____
_____
_____

One application of this lesson to my life: With God's help . . .

❑ I will stop worrying about _____

_____

and begin trusting God for_____

_____

❑ I will do what Jesus tells me to do, which I believe to be

_____

_____

_____

_____

_____

_____

❑ I will accept and embrace this _____
in my life and stop fighting _____

❑ other: _____

_____

_____

_____

_____

_____

_____

Walk the Word

❑ Observe what others do when they are disappointed.

❑ Notice another's reaction to you when you accept that
person without expectation or reservation.

❑ Observe how people tend to hold each other at arm's length.

Notes

Hearing His Heart

The following verses on this week's topic, "A Friend Is Accepting," are given for deepening your love for the Lord and for others. Space is provided after each verse for you to record your thoughts.

WEEK 1

Monday

Job 1:21

"'Naked I came from my mother's womb, and naked I will depart. The LORD gave and the LORD has taken away; may the

_____ *.'"*

_____

_____

_____

Tuesday

Jeremiah 42:6

"Whether it is favorable or unfavorable, we will obey the LORD our God, to whom we are sending you, so that it will go well with us, for we will _____ the LORD our God."

_____

_____

_____

Wednesday

Colossians 3:12-14

"As God's chosen people, holy and dearly loved, clothe yourselves with compassion, kindness, humility, gentleness and patience. _____ each other and forgive whatever grievances you may have against one another. Forgive as the Lord forgave you. And over all these virtues put on love, which binds them

all together in perfect unity."

_____

_____

_____

Thursday

1 Corinthians 13:4-7

"Love is patient, love is kind. It does not envy, it does not boast, it is not proud. It is not rude, it is _____ , it is not easily angered, it keeps no record of wrongs. Love does not delight in evil but rejoices with the truth. It always protects, always trusts, always hopes, always perseveres."

_____

_____

_____

Friday

2 Corinthians 6:11-12

"We have spoken freely to you, Corinthians, and opened wide our hearts to you. We are _____ our affection from you ...."

_____

_____

_____

WEEK 2

Monday

Romans 15:7

"Accept one another, then, just as Christ accepted you, in order to _____ ."

_____

_____

_____

Tuesday

John 13:20

"I tell you the truth, whoever accepts anyone I send accepts _____ ; and whoever accepts me accepts the One who sent me."

_____

_____

_____

Wednesday

Proverbs 17:17

"A friend loves at _____ times, and a brother is born for adversity."

_____

_____

_____

Thursday

Proverbs 19:20

"Listen to advice and _____ , and in the end you will be wise."

_____

_____

_____

Friday

Proverbs 10:8

"The _____ accept commands, but a chattering fool comes to ruin."

_____

_____

_____

Mary of Bethany
A Friend Gives Generously

"Do all the good you can
By all the means you can
In all the ways you can
In all the places you can
At all the times you can
To all the people you can
As long as ever you can."

—Jo Petty

Scripture Reading: Matthew 26:6-13,
Mark 14:1-11 and John 12:1-10

How does one express love to a friend? In this day when there are so many cheap imitations of love and friendship, how does one recognize a true friend? Let's take a sneak peek into Mr. Simon's home, where genuine and counterfeit friends have gathered for a time of celebration.

ry to imagine that you have been invited to attend a by-invitation-only dinner party at which your Friend, Jesus, is being honored. To have been invited means you are considered to be among His closest friends. At this point in His public ministry, He is limiting His contacts with people. No longer can He freely and publicly circulate as He did before (John 11:54). His assassins are stalking Him. Instead, Jesus must quietly go about His everyday commitments with as little fanfare as possible. This dinner itself is a rather secretive occasion, and the plan is to keep the occasion low-key. However, that plan is about to be drastically altered. What happens is unexpected by nearly everyone. What was planned to be a quiet, intimate dinner party is soon to turn into a lavish and unforgettable celebration!

As you enter Simon's home, there are several things you observe. First, the atmosphere is charged with emotion. Those gathered are Jesus' friends, and they tend to be people of passion. Their feelings about a given subject quickly surface, and Jesus certainly has a way of drawing out those emotions. Love. Hatred. Sadness. Greed. Unselfishness. Laughter. They're all in the open for everyone to see.

Next, you notice the personalities. The guests represent quite a mixed bag, but Jesus is a Friend to all of them. How He loves His friends, and most of them love Him, too. Mary, Martha, and Lazarus are among those assembled. Judas too mingles among the guests, but he has a markedly different agenda from the others. He is walking tall and feeling mighty fine. He has things to say that he thinks others should take note of, and he often gives away a piece of his mind that he really should keep. He is a polished talker but an inept listener. Soon he will fail another hearing test that will ultimately prove deadly.

Finally, your roving eyes catch a glimpse of the Guest of Honor, Jesus. It is easy to see from His expressions that His emotions are mixed. On the one hand, He is delighted to be in the company of friends. He has a lot on His mind and wants to be surrounded by those who care for Him and support Him as His hour of darkness approaches.

On the other hand, you notice almost immediately that He doesn't feel much like partying. His spirit is weighed down with a heavy burden. He knows that His days on earth are numbered and that He will very soon face torturous death by crucifixion. Even though He has broached the subject several times, no one seems to comprehend either His words or His pain.

Well, maybe there is an exception. There does seem to be at least one who has discerned what is going on. She's the one who sits at His feet whenever she can. This evening, as He reclines while dining, she is right there at His feet. Mary of Bethany is her name, and loving is her game.

At last the dinner bell rings. Martha is characteristically clanging pottery and pans; the guests are enjoying the food, the ambiance, and the lively chatter; and Mary, as usual, is listening. The air is pungent with a variety of blended aromas: the smells of freshly baked garlic bread, Galilean fish filets, fig mousse, seaweed salad with olive oil dressing—and Parfum du Bethany. Uh, excuse me! Perfume? Where did that come from? Are you actually detecting perfume, or could your imagination be playing tricks on you? It is a rich, exotic fragrance, and it is permeating the atmosphere.

Suddenly the room becomes quiet. The chatter and clatter cease, and all eyes focus on Jesus. He is transfixed with the one who is kneeling and pouring (not dabbing) perfume on His head and feet, and then wiping it with her long tresses of hair. For a moment, heaven seems to stand still. Earth is quiet too, at least in this household, as the truth of the incarnation is being reenacted before everyone's eyes.

This lavish outpouring by Mary is symbolic of the boundless giving of the Father in sending His Son to pour out His love upon creation. Mary, sitting at Jesus' feet, understands this incredible love offering to the world. She may be the only one who understands its essence, because she is the only one who consistently sits at His feet listening to His heart and catching His vision. Surely Jesus is touched. The cost of this perfume is equal to more than a year's wages. Mary must love Him incredibly to sacrifice so much.

Through Mary's quiet gesture the Good News of the Gospel is beautifully portrayed and *taught*, but unfortunately, this night it is not *caught*. Many criticize Mary in low undertones. And Judas has the audacity to disparage her action openly: *"Why this waste of perfume? It could have been sold for more than a year's wages and the money given to the poor"* (John 12:5). His words are deceptively pious, for his intentions of embezzlement plainly fail to match his platitudes about caring for the poor. Excusing himself from the party, the betrayer immediately hustles off to the religious leaders to join them in their plot to kill Jesus.

What a striking contrast between a true friend and a counterfeit friend. The one is committed to giving, in this case wordlessly, to others, while the other is committed to using the strategy of words to cover up what he has no intention of giving. Judas is talking, but certainly not walking, love. Mary, on the other hand, is walking (and kneeling) in love because she is listening to Love, in the person of Jesus Christ, whom the Father has sent.

So *"be imitators of God, therefore, as dearly loved children and live a life of love, just as Christ loved us and gave Himself up for us as a fragrant offering and sacrifice to God"* (Ephesians 5:1-2). Genuine friends listen and in listening connect with you. They invite relationship. False friends react, run, and detach themselves from you when the going gets tough. They destroy relationship.

The dinner party finally comes to an end, but the sweet fragrance lingers on and on. Jesus carries it with Him to Pilate's torture chamber as He is stripped of His clothes, beard, skin, and dignity. Mary carries it with her on her hair and returns sweet hugs to those who come to comfort her in her mourning. Simon's house will long be bathed in the scent that he will always associate with this evening.

An ordinary dinner party to honor one Guest has ultimately turned into a surprise party to honor many. How, you ask, can this be true? Mary had thought she would surprise Jesus. Actually, Jesus had quite a surprise for Mary. For the next two thousand years and beyond, this beautiful story would be told and retold in her honor. But, she would say, the retelling has been in *His* honor, in tribute to the One whose blood was soon to be poured out, who was poured out for her, and for me and for you. Does it come as a surprise to hear of His lavish love for you? So tell me, friend, whose surprise party is this?

A Modern Day Story
Cindy: A Friend Who Gives Generously

"I had asked the Lord to be my Savior when I was a young child and I had grown up in the church learning about the Lord, but for many years I had failed to apply what I learned in a practical way to my life. It was as I saw how patiently the Lord had pursued me, how He had drawn me to Himself for many, many years that my heart truly became tender toward serving Him. I had always known that *'God so loved the world that He gave His one and only Son, that whoever believes in Him shall not perish, but have eternal life'* (John 3:16). Now I knew that God so loved Cindy that He gave His one and only Son. Do you see the difference? I had known that He had died for the world which included me, but had not personalized that to realize He died for me individually.

"As my heart became more responsive to His love, His patience, His long-suffering, His gentleness, and His kindness toward me, it became my natural response to desire to serve Him. I also came to realize how much time had been wasted in selfish pursuits, in things that had very little eternal consequence. When I asked myself what I had done to repay the love and sacrifice Christ had made for me, the answer was, *'very little.'* And here I was, with probably more than half my life lived, and for what? Those thoughts compelled me to begin making my life count for Him and to say yes to anything He asked me to do."

I have often been softened by Cindy's tenderness for others and the unusual way she accepts people and sees their worth and value. I can call her in the middle of the day, even when things are hectic at work, and she always has a kind word to say about someone, and an encouraging word to say to me. She leaves *a lingering fragrance* when I hang up the phone.

Sharing Our Hearts

Discussion Starters

Reflect on the following thoughts we will discuss together. Take particular note of those that strike a chord with you and add notes in the margin about them.

1. What determines your standard for giving?

   ❏ how others give to me

   ❏ how Jesus gives to me

   ❏ how I want others to give to me

   ❏ whatever feels good or right at the moment

   ❏ whatever is convenient or easy

   ❏ other: _____

   _____

   _____

   _____

   _____

2. Jesus said that Mary did what she could (Mark 14:8). What could she do?

   ❏ give her heart

   ❏ offer her total life savings

   ❏ listen more than talk

   ❏ stay close to Him

   ❏ other: _____

   _____

   _____

   _____

3. How is that different from saying that Mary did what she *should*?

- ❏ not as legalistic sounding
- ❏ doesn't leave a sense of guilt because she hasn't done enough
- ❏ indicates that she is acting out of love, not out of obligation
- ❏ emphasizes that she doesn't have to meet anyone else's expectations for giving
- ❏ other: _____

  _____

  _____

  _____

4. When you are pouring out your friendship, love, and resources, how can you safeguard against depletion?

- ❏ keep refilling at the feet of Jesus
- ❏ other _____

  _____

  _____

  _____

  _____

  _____

5. What factors can combine to cause a friendship to dissolve?

- ❏ talking too much
- ❏ breaking a confidence
- ❏ refusing to forgive

❏ taking friendship for granted
❏ failing to listen to what is really being said
❏ being too busy
❏ being selfish
❏ other _____

_____
_____
_____
_____
_____

6. What qualities and actions combine to form a lasting, genuine friendship?

❏ faithfulness

❏ honesty

❏ guarding confidentiality

❏ staying in touch regularly

❏ remembering

❏ praying

❏ forgiving

❏ sharing joys and hurts together

❏ other _____

_____
_____
_____
_____
_____

A Change of Heart

Lesson Summary and Application

One main thought I have gleaned from the lesson:

_____

_____

_____

_____

One application of this lesson to my life: With God's help . . .

- ❏ I will be more generous in my giving.
- ❏ I will be aware of those ways in which God gives generously to me every day.
- ❏ I will be generous in my words and actions to my friend, _____ , this week.
- ❏ other: _____

_____

_____

_____

Walk the Word

- ❏ Watch how someone goes the extra mile to love you.
- ❏ Think about what it feels like to receive an expensive gift.
- ❏ Risk being generous rather than being safe and stingy.

Notes

Make Me An Instrument of Your Peace

Lord, make me an instrument of your peace.
Where there is hatred, let me sow love.
Where there is injury, pardon.
Where there is doubt, faith.
Where there is despair, hope.
O Divine Master,
Grant that I may not so much seek
To be consoled, as to console.
To be understood, as to understand.
To be loved, as to love.
For it is in giving, that we receive.
It is in pardoning that we are pardoned.
It is in dying that we are born
To Eternal Life.

—St. Francis of Assisi

Hearing His Heart

The following verses on this week's topic, "A Friend Gives Generously," are given for deepening your love for the Lord and for others. Space is provided after each verse for you to record your thoughts.

FINAL WEEK

Monday

Proverbs 11:24-25

*"One man gives freely, yet _____ ;
another withholds unduly, but comes to _____ .
A generous man will prosper; he who refreshes others will himself be refreshed."*

_____

_____

_____

Tuesday

Psalm 112:5

*"Good will come to him who is _____ and
lends freely, who conducts his affairs with justice."*

_____

_____

_____

Wednesday

1 Timothy 6:18

*"Command them to do good, to be _____
_____ , and to be _____
and willing to share."*

_____

_____

_____

Thursday

2 Corinthians 9:7

"*Each man should _____ what he has decided in his heart to _____, not reluctantly or under compulsion, for God loves a cheerful giver.*"

_____

_____

_____

Friday

Romans 12:6-8

"*We have different _____ , according to the grace given us. If a man's gift is prophesying, let him use it in proportion to his faith. If it is serving, let him serve; if it is teaching, let him teach; if it is encouraging, let him encourage; if it is contributing to the needs of others, let him _____ ; if it is leadership, let him govern diligently; if it is showing mercy, let him do it cheerfully.*"

_____

_____

_____

_____

_____

_____

_____

_____

Prayer Journal

Lesson 1   Date _____

PRAISES

_____
_____
_____
_____
_____
_____
_____
_____
_____

PETITIONS

_____
_____
_____
_____
_____
_____
_____
_____
_____

Prayer Journal

Lesson 2   Date _____

PRAISES

_____
_____
_____
_____
_____
_____
_____
_____
_____
_____

PETITIONS

_____
_____
_____
_____
_____
_____
_____
_____
_____
_____

Prayer Journal

Lesson 3   Date _____

PRAISES

_____
_____
_____
_____
_____
_____
_____
_____
_____
_____

PETITIONS

_____
_____
_____
_____
_____
_____
_____
_____
_____
_____

Prayer Journal

Lesson 4   Date _____

PRAISES

_____
_____
_____
_____
_____
_____
_____
_____
_____
_____

PETITIONS

_____
_____
_____
_____
_____
_____
_____
_____
_____
_____

Prayer Journal

Lesson 5   Date _____

PRAISES

_____
_____
_____
_____
_____
_____
_____
_____
_____
_____

PETITIONS

_____
_____
_____
_____
_____
_____
_____
_____
_____
_____

Prayer Journal

Lesson 6   Date _____

PRAISES

_____
_____
_____
_____
_____
_____
_____
_____
_____
_____

PETITIONS

_____
_____
_____
_____
_____
_____
_____
_____
_____
_____

Prayer Journal

Lesson 7   Date _____

PRAISES

_____
_____
_____
_____
_____
_____
_____
_____
_____
_____

PETITIONS

_____
_____
_____
_____
_____
_____
_____
_____
_____
_____

Poem Credits

The poem, "To A New Friend," credited to Margaret Clarkson, was used by permission of M.E. Clarkson.

The poem, "He Maketh No Mistake," credited to A.M. Overton, was used by permission of Dr. Roberson and Gloria Shadowens, Tennessee Temple University.

The poem, "Make Me an Instrument of Your Peace," credited to St. Francis of Assisi, was used by permission of Doubleday Publishers.

The poem, "Profit and Loss," credited to Ron Jensen, was used by permission.

The poem, "Guests," credited to Martha Snell Nicholson, was taken from *Come Before Winter*, copyright © 1985 by Charles Swindoll, Inc., and was used by permission of Zondervan Publishing House.

The material credited to Paul Tournier in *To Understand Each Other* was used by permission of Westminster John Knox Press.

The material credited to Jo Petty from the book *Apples of Gold* was used by permission of The C. R. Gibson Company.

The material from *A Mother's Touch*, credited to Kathy Erickson, copyright © 1998 by Tehabi Books and MOPS International, was used by permission of Zondervan Publishing House.

The material from *A Silver Pen For Cloudy Days*, credited to Susan Lenzkes, copyright © 1987 by Zondervan Publishing House, was used by permission of Discovery House Publishers, Grand Rapids, Michigan.

Note to the Reader

The publisher invites you to share your response to the message of this book by writing Discovery House Publishers, P.O. Box 3566, Grand Rapids, MI 49501, USA or by calling 1-800-653-8333. For information about other Discovery House publications, contact us at the same address and phone number. Find us on the Internet at http://www.dhp.org/ or send e-mail to books@dhp.org.

The design of this study guide is based on the tools used in the ministry of Friendship Circle® International. If you would like more information please contact: Friendship Circle® International, P.O. Box 2062, Renton, WA 98056.